THE STOIC GENTLEMAN

100 Guided Principles For Modern Men

CW01189306

Tony Gillis

THE STOIC GENTLEMAN

PALMETTO
PUBLISHING
Charleston, SC
www.PalmettoPublishing.com

Copyright © 2024 by Tony Gillis

All rights reserved

No portion of this book may be reproduced, stored in a retrieval system, or transmitted in any form by any means–electronic, mechanical, photocopy, recording, or other–except for brief quotations in printed reviews, without prior permission of the author.

Paperback ISBN: 9798822961326

Introduction

In a world filled with distractions, uncertainties, and constant changing demands, the pursuit of success can often feel like navigating through rough waters without a compass. Yet, amidst the chaos of modern life, there exists a timeless philosophy that offers a guiding light, a philosophy that has withstood the test of time and continues to inspire and empower individuals to achieve greatness.

Welcome to "100 Stoic Principles for becoming your best Men." In this transformative journey, we dive into the wisdom of modern and stoic philosophy Stoicism, with its emphasis on self-mastery, resilience, and virtue, provides a blueprint for living a life of purpose, integrity, and fulfillment.

As men striving for success in various aspects of our lives whether it be it career, relationships, or personal development, we can pull valuable lessons from the Stoic philosophy. Through the exploration of 100 timeless principles, we uncover insights, strategies, and practices that empower us as men to overcome obstacles, cultivate resilience, and embrace the challenges that life presents.

Each principle serves as a guiding beacon, illuminating the path towards success and inner fulfillment.

From the cultivation of wisdom and the practice of self-discipline to the embrace of adversity and the pursuit of virtue, the Stoic principles offer a holistic framework for navigating the complexities of the modern world with clarity, purpose, and strength.

As you join me on this journey through "100 Stoic Principles for Successful Men," I invite you to approach each principle with an open mind and a willingness to introspect, reflect, and apply its teachings to your own life. May this book serve as a companion and a source of inspiration as you strive to realize your full potential and lead a life of excellence, integrity, and true success.

Embrace the wisdom of the Stoics, and let it guide you on your quest towards becoming the man you aspire to be.

The Common Man

In today's society, the common man must create an adaptive environment characterized by advanced technology, world uncertainties, and society shifts. With the fast paced of information and the increasing challenges of daily issues, staying informed has become essential. The common man must frequently seek out reliable sources of information, evaluate what is learned, and learn to make informed decisions that impact both his personal life as well as his professional life.

The common man must embrace adaptability as a core skill in facing the challenges of the modern world. Whether it's adapting to changes in his job, technology changes or shifts in social norms, flexibility is key to thriving in non-stop environments. This goes beyond professional life to personal relationships, where men must navigate diverse perspectives, embrace diversity, and develop empathy to have an understanding and put all the pieces together in a fast paced world.

The common man must prioritize holistic well-being, incorporating physical, mental, and emotional health. With the pressures of modern life, maintaining a healthy balance between work, leisure, and self-care is essential. Prioritizing mental health through stress management, seeking support when needed, and developing meaningful connections with others are essential practices for navigating through constant challenges of today's society with resilience and strength. By embracing these principles, the common man can strive for personal growth, contribute positively to his community, and navigate the challenges of today's modern world with confidence and integrity.

Control +Alt +Delete

- Control yourself.
- Alter Your Thinking.
- Delete Negative Thinking. Period!

Remember

The small details show that you truly care.

Collaborate when you can

This will often lead to better outcomes and more innovative solutions. If you have a specific project or idea in mind, feel free to share with ideal individuals and discuss how you might be able to collaborate on it.

Brother, every rejection, is just a redirection.

It doesn't matter where you come from

But what matters is that you are ready to live in the present now. It is never too late to reinvent yourself and reach your full potential. Take on new challenges and take the leap of faith today.

My brother, the key to true happiness, is to enjoy the present moments

Right now is where your power is, the past cannot be changed, and the future is hard to guess. You can control and act in this moment.

Remember this brother

The path of your ongoing growth is not based on what happens to you, but rather how you react to it.

Knowing yourself better

This is a greatly important part of learning. Being aware of your feelings, thoughts and behaviors, you will be able to see the parts of yourself where you can improve.

Practice moderation in all things my brother

As a man,

When you are both masculine, driven, a visionary, strong, as well as loving, kind, and understanding, that is what makes you a true powerful man.

You cannot have success

My brother, remember this, you cannot have success without purging, without process, with our sacrifices, sacrifice will have to become your companion and not your enemy.

Make it personal!

What you do behind closed matters. Align your personal life with your purpose. Don't just start with people connected with you, start it with you.

Prioritize

Prioritize, your most important tasks of the day. This will be key in developing healthy successful habits.

Waste no time disputing what a good man should be, be one!

Live with purpose

You will create lasting connections with people that could improve your life, increase your sense of worth in the world and overall help you feel valuable.

Do yourself a grand favor

Do yourself a grand favor, be 1% better than you were yesterday

My brother listen

My brother listen, it won't happen overnight, but if you quit it won't happen at all.

Take action today!

- Go after your dreams today!
- Get out of your comfort zone today!

Choose your circle wisely brother

Surround yourself with the right circle of friends, mentors, and colleagues, you can create a supportive environment that will help you with personal growth, success, and overall well-being.

Go get it

Rain, sleek or snow, still go get it!

Remember, true growth isn't about grand gestures

Remember, true growth isn't about grand gestures, more so the small consistent steps we take each day, push through doubts and have the courage to make a change.

Embrace the power of silence

My brother, embrace the power of silence. Allow your actions to speak louder than your words. Prioritizing action over excessive talking will lead to tangible results, meaningful progress, and effective communication. When you practice this it will demonstrate your intentions, values, and commitment to making a difference in what you create.

Develop a keen sense of the power of alignment

When certain events in your life just "flow", those just might me the actions steps to take towards a business adventure, an investment, or even a grand decision that can change your next few months or even a year.

Cultivate your demeanor

Do this by keeping yourself well groomed, choose an attire that fits you well, also that fits your personality. Practice healthy posture and walk with an upright confidence that tells the world you are ready to face whatever comes your way. Keep in ming brother, true essence of demeanor goes further than physical appearance, approach ever individual with sincerity and a gentleness.

Stick to the plan

Stick to the plan brother, you know it wasn't going to be easy.

Focus on building your confidence

Building your confidence will be essential for your personal growth and success.

Although this will be a gradual process, increasing your confidence will help you realize your full potential.

Do this by recognizing your strengths, set achievable goals, and push beyond your comfort zone.

Instead of seeking revenge, turn your attention into positive energy for success

This will be incredibly empowering for you brother. Focus on achieving your goals, excelling in your visions, and becoming the best version of yourself. Let your success be the ultimate response to any doubters or individuals who may have done you wrong.

Be kind to yourself my brother

This principle will be essential. Treat yourself with compassion, understanding, and patience,

especially during challenging times. Acknowledge your strengths and weaknesses without harsh judgment to yourself.

Use your pain

Use your pain, to push you into a place of abundance, use your pain into the foundation of your existence, breathing life into every moment.

Use your pain for fulfillment. Use your pain my brother.

Listen, when things are going well

You have to prepare for when things don't go so well. Here is how, stack away 20% for seasons of distress. By consistently setting aside a portion of your earnings, you can create a safety net to cover essential expenses and weather difficult times more comfortably. It's a smart financial strategy that helps build financial stability and resilience in the times of adversity.

Ask better questions

If you learn to ask better questions, you will discover better answers.

Create things to create your money

My brother you need to create things to create your money, it will take you time while you are in the creation phase, but eventually you will have your final product to show to the world.

Turn into an idea producer my brother

Do this by exploring diverse topics asking new ideas that can spark newer ideas. You can create inspiration from nature, art, or from other sources.

My brother, understand this key principle, "AMOR FATI"

A Latin phrase that means "love of fate" or "love of one's fate." Amor fati encourages you to embrace and accept your fate, whatever it may be, with love and gratitude. Rather than resisting or resenting the events that happen in your life, wholeheartedly embrace them, and recognizing that every experience, whether positive or negative, contributes to your growth and development.

Get comfortable with being uncomfortable

Brother, if you don't like where you are

Make a move, you are not a tree.

It is time to get hyper focused on yourself

Right here, right now it is time to get hyper focused on yourself, put yourself in a state of elevation, it's time to massively increase your productivity, increase your vitality, be relentless and go.

CAKE/USDT
CAKEUSDT, 1
Spot
Limit
Market
Buy CAKE
Sell CAKE
Price
Amount
Market Trades
My Trades
Market Activities
Order History
Trade History
Funds

Get comfortable with Talking with Strangers brother

This may be one of those most valuable principles you develop. Consistently carry a networking mindset and you will be astonished on the professional relationships you will build.

Figure out your mission statement

Your one sentence mission statement should be so powerful, that it could not be completed in your lifetime.

My brother, if you're not networking, you're stunting your professional growth

Mmake it a point to connect with individuals who are doing what you want to do, learn from mentors, surround yourself with people who are at a higher level than you, doing this you will develop great habits from highly successful people. This will be a crucial principle to implement as you grow.

Be present

As challenging as it may be, do your very best to be present. In the moment. When you're having a meaningful conversation be present, when you're talking with your significant other be present, when you're with your kids be present. Be present my brother.

Avoid multiple sex partners

Brother though this is a personal decision, keep in mind that ENGAGING with multiple sex partners, especially as you are on your journey, there will always be that one or two that will fight to defame your character, the chance of you developing envy towards you, and could be a health concern and so much more. Be very mindful of this principle to avoid self-sabotage.

Take action now

If you continue to wait for the right time, you will wait your entire life, and nothing will ever come of it. Take action now.

Be patient

The most powerful thing you can do right now brother, is be patient while things are unfolding, your time is coming.

My brother, learn to accept constructive criticism

This will be a valuable skill that can lead to personal and professional growth. Remain composed and open-minded when receiving feedback, even if it's difficult to hear.

Resist the urge to become defensive or make excuses

Instead, absorb the feedback with humility and a willingness to learn. Last, ask questions, get clarification if something is unclear or if you need more information to fully understand the feedback.

My brother, you very well might start to lose many of your close friends and family

As soon as you start to level up, and choose to be different, embrace it and push even harder.

Try to see your reflection in the other person's eyes

That's a great way to express that you are being attentive and empathetic during a meaningful conversation.To truly connect with the other person. This will also help you work on your active listening skills.

Not to take things so personally

When you learn to not take things so personally, you start to become more mature.

You're not going to feel good every single day

You're not going to feel good every single day, do it tired, do it sore, do it in rough times, this is when you truly start to grow.

Decide what kind of life you really want

My brother, decide what kind of life you really want and then say NO! to anything that isn't that.

Repetition will teach you everything

Repetition will teach you everything, you can honestly out work anything when you truly put your mind to it too.

Keep in mind brother

Keep in mind brother, you always have greater potential, no matter what others may have said to you, avoid becoming the standard and expectation of average, the average man inspires no one.

Today!

Make a promise to yourself to leave no stone unturned, get better every single day,

You must believe

My brother, if you're waking up every day and have a feeling that there has to be more than this, you must believe that there is and take that leap of faith.

Don't wish it

Don't wish it my brother, be it.

Fear is not real

My brother, fear is not real, but its true meaning is ...false evidence appearing real, do not allow the (feeling) of fear to cripple you, nothing can stand in your way with true determination.

Get your optimal sleep

Get your optimal sleep. Here is why it is key for you to get your sleep in as a man. It is crucial for your overall health, including mental and physical well-being. It plays a vital role in your cognitive function, emotional balance, and maintaining a healthy immune system. Make sure to take healthy necessary steps to optimize your sleep.

Make sure to practice empathy

As men we are held to a high standard of being stern, or "manlike", which is great. When you start to practice empathy it will build a further understanding of people, strengthen relationships, and usually creates a positive social environment. Be actively listening, considering others' perspectives,

My brother makes sure to wake with a purpose

put yourself in a situation where you have lots to lose, wake up knowing that whatever you are working on, it is going to bring value to the universe and the people you connect with.

Embrace the gray hairs

The moment you realize you're ready to take your life to the next level, is when you embrace the gray hairs. Except them as wisdom, except them as growth, except them as a new chapter of your new journey.

Practice Sexual Transmutation

Practice sexual transmutation, this just may be one of the most powerful personal principles you should commit to in your journey. If you haven't yet, read (think and grow rich) by napoleon hill, in there you will learn how powerful practicing sexual transmutation is and its importance as you are walking in your purpose.

If you are highly anxious

Listen brother, if you are highly anxious, you are probably thinking too much in the future, if you're stressed, you might be dwelling on the things you wish you could have changed in the past. Live in the moment today, and make the hard decisions for a more meaningful and fulfilling future.

Remember this

When faced with any decision in life, whether it be purchasing a new vehicle, signing a lease an apartment, buying a house investing in a business opportunity, a relationship take a pause and be calculated before making a final decision, this can be within minutes' hours or even days take your time my brother.

Embrace silence

Embrace silence as introspection and self-discovery

Reset. Restart. Refocus

Reset. Restart. Refocus. But don't you dare give up on your dreams.

Friendly reminder my brother

Anything that costs you your mental health is much too expensive.

Best times of your life

Remember, some of the best times of your life haven't even happened yet.

You survived too many storms

You survived too many storms to be bothered by tiny raindrops.

You must understand this

My brother, you must understand this, you do not get any do overs, once your day is over that's it, make the phone calls today, get in the gym today, start taking action on your Projects Today.

Read! Read!! Read!!!

Make small investments into books and audiobooks that help you with personal development, financial literacy, and physical health guidance.

Please do not rush the process

My brother, please do not rush the process, when you are in your (plating the seed) phase, allow it to take its course, no matter the time frame, taking your time is a precious gift.

FAITH
FORWARD
FUTURE
Moving past your disappointments, delays, and destructive thinking
CHAD VEACH

Build your life's action

Build your life's action by consistently taking action, a little action steps will take you a long way!

Create a habit to get up early

As hard as it may be, create a habit to get up early and attack your goals before the distractions of life take over, etc workouts, work on projects, get your clean nutrition in you.

Make sure to find an accountability partner

My brother, make sure to find an accountability partner, someone who will be open with you emotionally and energetically, invested in your true personal growth. This will be essential for your personal success.

Practice gratitude

On a daily basis, practice gratitude every single morning. Here are a few examples:

- I am grateful for my health
- I am grateful for waking up
- I am grateful for all the blessings in my life
- I am grateful for a roof over my head
- I am feeling grateful for the abundance in my life.

You need to learn from your consequences

My brother, you need to learn from your consequences, you have to take a hard mental evaluation on what's happening when you're not doing the moral things you're supposed to be doing. If you're noticing consistency of negative give back, then you must make the change, take responsibility, and work on doing better.

Remove All Negative Toxicity

This is going to be very important for you to take action on this brother. Understandable, this can be very challenging, but for your life to start opening up for you, you must remove any and all negative toxicity in your life whether it's certain family,environment, friends, unhealthy relationships, excessive drinking, pornography, self-sabotaging negative talk, i think you get the picture.

Make your mental health a priority

Heal as needed my brother, it's ok to seek help when needed, seeking help when needed isnt an act of weakness, but a great step to a more balanced and prosperous life. Try your best to prioritize your mental health as it goes on your journey. Act on this, as soon as you can, and your future self all thank you.

Take a mental note on this

Take a mental note on this, not everyone is really going to be on your side, there are others waiting for you to fail, don't let this happen.

Keep your circle small and take action.

My brother, keep this in mind

As you fight to become the best version of yourself, the constant life resistance will make you want to quit....

DONT!

Take extreme ownership

Take extreme ownership, by taking extreme ownership of your life it means fully embracing responsibility for your actions and outcomes, without making excuses or blaming others. It involves taking control of your life and decisions.

Get comfortable with investing

My brother, i know you want to become the absolute best version of yourself. Let me tell you get comfortable with investing, invest in mentorships, invest in education, invest in a new project you've been wanting to work on. Invest in that idea that's been running through your head, it doesn't have to break your bank, but take the calculated risk and invest in your future.

Don't let the distractions distract you.

Greatness takes time

My brother, if you feel that your process is slow, keep in mind that a slow process is a healing process. Greatness takes time to start to blossom.

Be bold

Be courageous, be relentless, and conduct your business!!

Enough is Enough

You must get to a point in your life where you say just that, enough! Is enough! You have to be tired of losing, you must be sick and tired of your draining environment, you must be fed up with being mediocre and ready to make the change, be the change.

Avoid the victim mentality

My brother, i get it, i know you're going through a lot of challenges in your life journey with others, not fully believing in you, and put you down specially, as a man, this here is your reminder to fight the victim mentality, do not let your current circumstances put you in a victim state of being and remind yourself every single day that you are a víctor and not a victim.

Avoid Overuse of Screen

Try your best to avoid excess use of the screen. This will put you at a sedentary lifestyle, resulting in unnecessary weight gain, negative effects on mental and physical health, as well as adapting to isolation. Your hormonal balance may be compromised with overuse of the screen time and result in drops your testosterone levels.

Have a Provider Mindset

My brother, they're ready for you. They're waiting for you, your family, your kids, your Partner, your loved ones, your friends, the unfortunate, they're all ready for you to blossom into be the provider you were created to be. Keep that mindset going and provide and grind.

You have to have Faith my brother

We all have our different beliefs, and what we believe in, but! You must have trust and Faith in a Higher power that what you are working towards, all your visions You are having, your main goals, will eventually happen. You must trust and believe that even when you go through the roughest seasons, you will reach your full potential

Practice your Alpha self

Practicing your alpha self will help you build confidence, assertiveness, and effective communication skills, contributing to personal and professional growth. It involves building leadership qualities and a strong sense of self-assurance.

Avoid self sabotage

At all cost, avoid self sabotage my brother, this is what will happen when you focus on avoiding self-sabotage. You will create a foundation for personal and professional success. You're more likely to achieve your major goals, experience improved mental well-being, build stronger relationships, and maintain a positive outlook in various aspects of your life. This is key.

Make healthy sacrifices

The magic you are looking for in your life, comes from the work you are not doing. Get in the right community, be generous, make healthy sacrifices, confront your fears my brother, and execute.

Live your life of Purpose

My brother, avoid going through life as a wanderer, be a man of action, be a man of risk taking, go through your journey with heavy purpose and level up.

Take a step back, breathe

When life throws you curveballs, and it will my brother, take a step back, breathe. And think about how you can respond with wisdom and strength, that is where your true resilience is developed.

Learn the power of NO

You must learn that in certain situations it is ok just to say no. The power of saying no is necessary for setting boundaries and prioritizing your time and energy. It will also allow you to focus on tasks that contribute to your well-being and success, creating a healthier internal balance and preventing burnout.

Everyone sees the product of your current success

Most of the time, everyone sees the product of your current success you have now, but most won't know how long it took, or what it took to be where you are today. Consistently work on your craft behind the scenes, and when time is ready, bring your product to the stage.

Consider your daily choices

Make sure they align with your long term goals and values.

Prioritize your essentials

My brother, keep in mind to prioritize your essentials, and eliminate the nonsense.

Practice your self-discipline

Take control of your emotions, your actions and decisions, you don't have to control or manipulate others, just be in charge of your own life.

Protect your time

Your time is your most precious resource, and once it's gone, you can't make any more of it. Guard your time like you guard your most valuable possessions.

My brother, do the hard things

If it's more challenging than what you're used to, do it! The next time you come across something challenging or hard, lean into it and remind yourself that adversity is what will create your true character.

Make people around you better

This will be another path of happiness for you, it's about being an inspiration to those who look up to you, knowingly and unknowingly.

Take the time each day and reflect

Reflect on your thoughts, actions and decisions, this is crucial for your self-development. If needed, you can make personal changes to becoming your ideal self.

Be committed to your race

When you are running your race be committed to your race, do not be committed to excuses, be committed to crossing that finish line.

Get better my brother.

Your Life gets better only when you get better.

Practice a strong mindset

It is important for my brother to practice a strong mindset. Train your mind to work with solutions instead of the problems. When start to build yourself with a strong mindset, you become much better at facing adversity instead of negativity approaching a situation.

Pay attention to the law of alignment

As you navigate through your journey, have a keen since on what is working for you with ease. If you notice you are constantly hitting a wall when you're working on projects, connections or even partnerships, that may be an indication to take a different calculated approach, and allow things to just "Flow".

Know your value

My brother, knowing your value is crucial for self-awareness and confidence. It will you make informed decisions, set boundaries, and pursue opportunities that align with your worth and principles.

Avoid procastination at all cost

When you procrastinate this will lead to delayed tasks, that need your attention. Procrastination will also contribute to heightened stress levels due to feeling rushed and last minute decisions. Completely avoiding procrastination is challenging, but including strategies like setting realistic goals, breaking tasks into smaller steps, and maintaining a schedule can help minimize its impact.

If you lack focus, you lack everything.

Detach yourself from materialism

My brother. Instead of pouring energy into the external, focus on your experience, your relationships, and personal growth. Reflect on what truly brings fulfillment and consider minimizing to simplify your life.

AMOR FATI

A key principle to live by brother. Stated by marcus aurelius. Simply means "love of fate". This is a concept emphasizing embracing and accepting everything that happens in life, both positive and negative, with love and gratitude.

Avoid seeking external approval

This is crucial for building genuine self-worth and inner stability. When you solely rely on others validation, it can lead to a constant need for external validation, making your self-esteem vulnerable to the opinions of others. Build motivation and confidence allowing for a more authentic and fulfilling sense of accomplishment.

Build your Ability

As a man, you must build your ability to maintain composure with negative emotions.

Don't stop

Don't stop until you are extremely proud of what you have achieved.

Avoid dwelling on past mistakes

Avoiding this will allow you to maintain mental well-being, learn from your challenging experiences, and focus on present opportunities for growth and improvement. It's a healthy mindset to just move forward.

Make self-care a priority

Make self-care a priority in your waking journey my brother. Go to the gym, maintain a clean balanced nutrition plan, get monthly athletic massages, as well as taking care of your external appearance, like your skin and clean apparel. These principles are highly crucial for you as an high performing man because it will maintain your physical and mental well-being, allowing you to be more resilience to stress, and most importantly, it will set a great example for your family and peers.

Make a point to Prioritize your Daily tasks

For the father's, make a point to prioritize your daily tasks, delegate your responsibilities, and most importantly, as hard as it is for us as men, create clear communication with your family on your goals and personal expectations, this is essential for balance and understanding.

You have no time for gossip

My brother, you have no time for gossip, drama, respect your time and energy, and be cautious of what content or any negative conversions that you happen to be involved in, it's ok to step away when necessary.

Make sure to embrace continuous learning

My brother makes sure to embrace continuous learning. Learning is a lifelong journey, every piece of learning allows you to adapt to the fast pace changes of the world. Read, seek out new skills, or even pick up a form of self-defense.

Maintain high morals

Maintain high morals for yourself-brother, even when you think no one is watching, they are watching, to help with this, act daily as if someone who you highly respect, is watching your every move, this will keep you at a high honorable favor.

Keep going!

I have yet to meet a strong and successful man who has not gone through heavy adversity in his life, if this is you now, i'm here to tell you, keep going!

Keep your major goals and visions to yourself

My brother, keep your major goals and visions to yourself, if you must share, share to the very few select that will actually see and value your vision, someone who has been genuine with you from the start, someone you could truly trust with your dreams in their hands. This is vital to protect because it will help avoid external judgment or negativity that might hinder your motivation. It will also maintain a level of privacy, allowing you to work on your goals without the pressure of others expectations.

Make it a priority and habit to note down

Make it a priority and habit to note down when you get an "AH-HA" moment. This is when you get a sudden realization or when a great idea comes to your mind. This is important especially when you are in the creative stage of your ideas and projects. Noting your light bulb ideas will allow you to revisit your idea giving you clarity and motivation to take action on it as you go.

Internally say what you want to be

Do what you Have to do to obtain it.

Any person capable of angering you becomes your master

Brother, any person capable of angering you becomes your master, they can anger you only when you allow it.

Work for your gift

When you find your gift, work for your gift brother, and exhaust every option possible where you can expand and grow around what you do.

Be wise on who you allow in your inner circle

The company you keep can greatly influence your thoughts, actions, and overall well-being. Choose those who uplift and inspire you, Creating a positive and growth-oriented environment.

Seek Challenge my brother

Real growth happens when we embark in to challenges and step outside our comfort zones. Embracing discomfort and learning from adversity will build in personal and intellectual growth.

Your time is like a treasure my brother

Spend it wisely on pursuits that bring fulfillment, joy, and contribute positively to your life and the lives of others. Time is a precious resource.

Empower others for happiness my brother

Doing this not only spreads joy but creates a ripple effect, fostering a more positive and supportive team around you.

Be thankful for the small joys

My brother, be thankful for the small joys, and the big wins, as gratitude for both the little moments and major achievements cultivates a mindset of appreciation, bringing balance and contentment to life.

Keep in mind my brother

A small act of kindness creating a world effect too.

VOLUNTEER

When you are in moments in distress

Keep in mind that this too shall pass.

Avoid comparing yourself to others

At all cost, avoid comparing yourself to others, everyone's journey is so unique, and comparing yourself to others can undermine your self-worth and hinder personal growth. Focus on your personal growth my brother.

Take calculated risk

Take calculated risk, as calculated risks, followed by thoughtful thinking, can lead to opportunities for growth and success that might otherwise remain undiscovered.

The trap of overthinking can paralyze your progress

My brother Overthinking may hinder your action and progress. Find a balance between thoughtful consideration and taking strategic steps forward to avoid the paralysis of overthinking.

Practice the power of being Present

This is a key principle embracing the present moment enhances mindfulness, enriching your experiences and fostering a deeper connection with yourself and others.

Burnout is real

My brother, a couple ways to recognize it and prevent it is

Continuous persistence of knowledge.

Remember, the key to a fulfilling lifestyle, is the continuous persistence of knowledge.

Your net worth is your network.

Keep this in mind brother

Everything is temporary my brother

Understand that all tough times are short lived, in challenging times, Except what you cannot control.

Consistency is key.

Embrace vulnerability

As men we are used to seeing vulnerability as weakness, let's debunk that and see it as an act of courage, a willingness to admit your imperfections and confront your flaws. Allow yourself to be vulnerable and allow authenticity in your life.

Embrace failure as a valuable learning experience

My brother when you think of the word (FAIL), Cease to make the fear of failure disrupt your dreams. Understand that failure really stands for (First, Attempt, In Learning). Embrace failure as a valuable learning experience. It provides insights, fosters resilience, and can be a stepping stone to growth and success.

SPACE FOR REFLECTION NOTES

END BOOK

As a high-performing man, optimal functioning is not just desirable, it's essential. In the pursuit of success and excellence, our ability to function at our best, both mentally and physically, directly impacts our performance, productivity, and overall well-being.

From the boardroom to the gym, from personal relationships to professional endeavors, our capacity to function effectively defines our ability to meet challenges head-on, adapt to changing circumstances, and achieve our goals with clarity and purpose.

To function at our peak, we must prioritize self-care, maintaining a balance between work and rest, challenge and recovery. This means nourishing our bodies with nutritious food, prioritizing regular exercise, and ensuring adequate sleep and relaxation.

Here are 20 Natural Supplements shown to help with the vitality, virility, and testosterone in men.

Caution!

(It is important to note that the effectiveness of these supplements can vary from person to person, and consulting with a healthcare professional before starting any new supplement regimen is highly recommended.)

- *Ashwagandha:* An adaptogenic herb that may help reduce cortisol levels and support testosterone production.
- *Tribulus Terrestris:* A plant extract believed to enhance libido and support Testosterone levels.
- *Fenugreek:* Contains compounds that may help increase testosterone levels and improve libido.
- *Ginger:* Contains gingerol, which may stimulate testosterone production.
- *DHEA (Dehydroepiandrosterone):* A hormone precursor that may support testosterone production, especially in older men.
- *Zinc:* An essential mineral involved in testosterone production and sperm health.
- *Vitamin D:* Plays a role in testosterone production, and deficiency is associated with low testosterone levels.
- *Magnesium:* Supports overall health and may help increase testosterone levels, especially in athletes and older adults.
- *Boron:* A trace mineral that may help increase free testosterone levels.

- *Vitamin K2:* Supports bone and cardiovascular health, and may also help increase testosterone levels.
- *Saw Palmetto:* Believed to inhibit the conversion of testosterone to dihydrotestosterone (DHT), thus helping to maintain higher testosterone levels.
- *Nettle Root:* Contains compounds that may help increase free testosterone levels by binding to sex hormone-binding globulin (SHBG).
- *Mucuna Pruriens:* A tropical legume containing L-dopa, which may support testosterone production and improve mood.
- *Ginseng:* An adaptogenic herb that may help reduce stress and support testosterone levels.
- *D-Aspartic Acid:* Amino acid that may help regulate testosterone synthesis in the testes.
- *Creatine:* A compound found in muscle cells that may help increase testosterone levels, especially in conjunction with resistance training.
- *Vitamin B6:* Plays a role in testosterone production and may help regulate hormone levels.
- *Oyster Extract:* Rich in zinc and other nutrients that support testosterone production.
- *Pumpkin Seed:* Contains phytosterols, which may help support testosterone levels.
- *Eurycoma Longifolia (Tongkat Ali):* A plant extract believed to support testosterone production and improve libido.

Again, before starting any new supplement regimen, it's essential to consult with a healthcare professional, especially if you have any underlying health conditions or are taking medications. Additionally, focusing on overall health through a balanced diet, regular exercise, stress management, and adequate sleep can also support healthy vitality levels.

As the final pages of this book draw to a close, I encourage you my friend, to carry on with these powerful principles into your daily existence. Allow these principles' to be a guide against the midst of life's challenges and uncertainties. Embrace each moment with clarity and composure, knowing that true strength lies in mastering your own mind and spirit. May the wisdom of "The Stoic Gentleman" empower you to navigate through the trials and flow of your life with grace, dignity, and inner peace.

I invite you to pause and reflect on the mighty impact of these daily principles and upon your life. As you stand at the face of a new beginning, I encourage you to embrace adversity as an opportunity for growth and let go of any obstacles that are beyond your control with acceptance. I wish that these whispers of stoicism would resonate within your heart, guiding you towards a life of purpose, integrity, and virtue.

Let the virtues of courage, wisdom, and self-discipline be your constant friend on your journey towards personal transformation and enlightenment. Embrace the challenges of life with stoic principles, knowing that within every trial lies an opportunity for growth and renewal.

Lastly, I will say this, you must carry on the momentum of this book's wisdom with trust, knowing that within the depths of your being is the key to lasting peace and contentment. Until next time my brother and may the spirit of stoicism guide you on your journey towards a life of purpose, virtue, and unyielding strength.

Milton Keynes UK
Ingram Content Group UK Ltd.
UKHW050706141024
449707UK00001B/6
9798822961326